Snow

by Grace Hansen

abdopublishing.com

Published by Abdo Kids, a division of ABDO, PO Box 398166, Minneapolis, Minnesota 55439.

Copyright © 2016 by Abdo Consulting Group, Inc. International copyrights reserved in all countries. No part of this book may be reproduced in any form without written permission from the publisher.

Printed in the United States of America, North Mankato, Minnesota.

052015

092015

Photo Credits: iStock, Shutterstock

Production Contributors: Teddy Borth, Jennie Forsberg, Grace Hansen

Design Contributors: Laura Rask, Dorothy Toth

Library of Congress Control Number: 2014958618

Cataloging-in-Publication Data

Hansen, Grace.

 Snow / Grace Hansen.

  p. cm. -- (Weather)

ISBN 978-1-62970-933-8

Includes index.

1. Snow--Juvenile literature.   I. Title.

551--dc23

                2014958618

Table of Contents

Cold Clouds

Snow comes from clouds.

Not all clouds make snow.

Only snow clouds make it.

Snow clouds are very cold. Like all clouds, they have water in them. The water forms **ice crystals**.

7

Snowflakes Make Snow

The ice crystals grow bigger. They become heavier. Then they fall from the snow cloud.

9

Ice crystals bump into each other on their way down. They clump together to make snowflakes.

Snow is made of snowflakes.

Snowflakes are made of water and lots of air.

Snowflakes have six sides.

But no two snowflakes

look just the same.

Snowflakes

15

Snow Keeps Things Warm

Snow is important. Winter can be very cold. Animals and plants need snow to stay warm.

17

Snow traps heat under the ground. Animals sleep in underground homes in the winter. Snow helps keep their homes warm. **Roots** and plants also need this warmth.

Snow in Springtime

Snow **melts** in the spring. It turns to water. The fresh water fills bodies of water. It also helps plants and trees bloom and grow.

20

21

The Water Cycle

Condensation

Precipitation

Evaporation

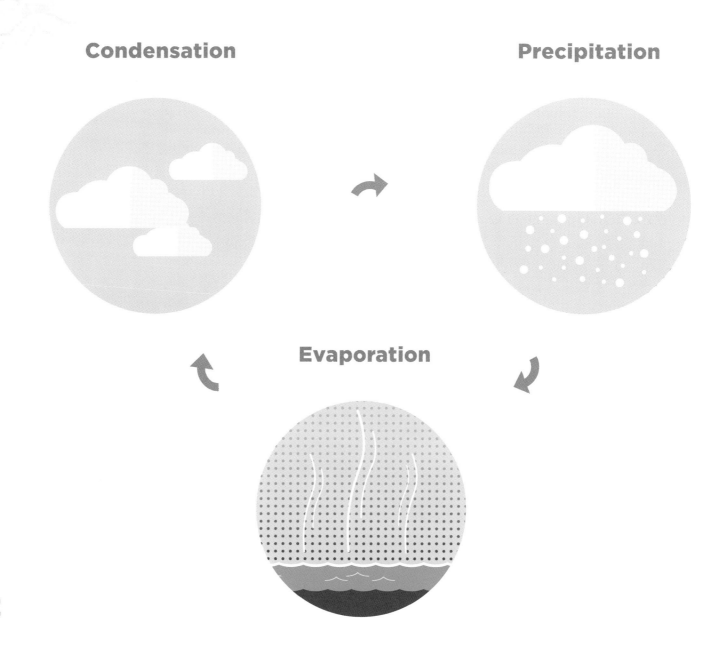

22

Glossary

ice crystal – a slowly falling crystal of ice. They clump together to make snowflakes.

melt – to change from a solid to a liquid state. This is usually from heat.

root – a part of a plant that, usually, grows downward into the soil. It holds the plant in place and gets water from the soil.

Index

abdokids.com

Use this code to log on to abdokids.com and access crafts, games, videos, and more!

Abdo Kids Code:
WSK9338